THE LITTLE BOOK OF
Family Group
Conferences
NEW ZEALAND STYLE

THE LITTLE BOOKS OF JUSTICE & PEACEBUILDING

Published titles include:

The Little Book of Restorative Justice, by Howard Zehr

The Little Book of Conflict Transformation, by John Paul Lederach

The Little Book of Family Group Conferences, New-Zealand Style,
by Allan MacRae and Howard Zehr

The Little Book of Strategic Peacebuilding, by Lisa Schirch

The Little Book of Strategic Negotiation,
by Jayne Seminare Docherty

The Little Book of Circle Processes, by Kay Pranis

The Little Book of Contemplative Photography, by Howard Zehr

The Little Book of Restorative Discipline for Schools,
by Lorraine Stutzman Amstutz and Judy H. Mullet

The Little Book of Trauma Healing, by Carolyn Yoder

The Little Book of Biblical Justice, by Chris Marshall

The Little Book of Restorative Justice for People in Prison,
by Barb Toews

El Pequeño Libro De Justicia Restaurativa, by Howard Zehr

The Little Book of Cool Tools for Hot Topics,
by Ron Kraybill and Evelyn Wright

The Little Book of Dialogue for Difficult Subjects,
by Lisa Schirch and David Campt

The Little Books of Justice & Peacebuilding
present, in highly accessible form, key concepts and
practices from the fields of restorative justice, conflict transformation, and peacebuilding. Written by leaders in these
fields, they are designed for practitioners, students, and
anyone interested in justice, peace, and conflict resolution.
The Little Books of Justice & Peacebuilding
series is a cooperative effort between the Center for Justice
and Peacebuilding of Eastern Mennonite University (Howard
Zehr, Series General Editor) and publisher Good Books
(Phyllis Pellman Good, Senior Editor).

THE LITTLE BOOK OF
Family Group
Conferences
NEW ZEALAND STYLE

ALLAN MACRAE
& HOWARD ZEHR

Good Books

Intercourse, PA 17534
800/762-7171
www.GoodBooks.com

Cover photograph by Howard Zehr.

Design by Dawn J. Ranck

THE LITTLE BOOK OF FAMILY GROUP CONFERENCES,
NEW ZEALAND STYLE
Copyright © 2004 by Good Books, Intercourse, PA 17534
International Standard Book Number: 978-1-56148-403-4
Library of Congress Catalog Card Number: 2003027514

Library of Congress Cataloging-in-Publication Data

MacRae, Allan.
   The little book of family group conference : New Zealand style / Allan
MacRae & Howard Zehr.
       p. cm.
Includes bibliographical references and index.
   ISBN 1-56148-403-2 (pbk. : alk. paper)
   1. Juvenile justice, Administration of--New Zealand. 2. Restorative justice--
New Zealand. 3. Victims of crimes--Services for--New Zealand. 4. Juvenile
delinquents--Rehabilitation--New Zealand. I. Zehr, Howard. II. Title.
   HV9230.4.A5M23 2004
   364.36'0993--dc22
                                                         2003027514

Table of Contents

1.
Introduction

Allan: A story, but first some personal reflections

As I reflect on the Family Group Conferences I have facilitated, I am filled with emotion. These feelings come from the suffering I have witnessed but, more importantly, from the powerful processes of healing and forgiveness I have seen take place.

Having led over a thousand Family Group Conferences, I often find myself asking how anyone could cause such suffering for another person. As I facilitate Conferences where offenders hear the impact of their offending on victims and families, the answer becomes clear: even in attacks involving direct encounters with victims, offenders seldom realize the trauma they have inflicted. They do not grasp how difficult it is for victims to move on and to repair and reclaim their lives.

I have come to believe in Family Group Conferences because I have witnessed offenders having to face the impact they have had on people. I have seen healing come when they acknowledge the hurt they have caused, and when they struggle to correct what they can and take responsibility for what they cannot, through some form of compensation and apology.

The following story is about a 16-year-old boy who was charged with "rape times three" on the same victim, a 13-year-old girl. This story demonstrates how Conferences can deal with serious and complicated cases, and the power of practice based in principle.

As is so often the case, the offender—I'll call him Robert—had himself been the victim of pedophiles from the age of five. His mother would take him to meetings of pedophiles and participate in their activities. In short, this was a boy who had not experienced appropriate sexual boundaries.

Joanne, his victim, had also been a victim previously. Having been subjected to incest, she found only one method of coping within her power. She shut down when under attack, allowing her mind to escape her body as best she could.

Robert and Joanna both ended up living in the same home as longer-term plans were being made for their care. Before long, Robert approached Joanna in her room. When he made sexual advances, Joanna responded the only way she knew; she closed down. When he didn't receive physical or verbal rejection, Robert returned twice more, although it was clear that he had not received any encouragement.

When I visited Joanna to explain her rights, I did so with the support of her caregiver and social worker. After hearing her rights, Joanna said she wanted to view the Conference but not be in the same room as the offender. I arranged for the Conference to be held in one room while she watched it through a video monitor in the next room. I suggested that she may want to have a representative in the room with the offender to speak for her. Joanna proposed that her caregiver represent her in the Conference while she observed from outside with an adult woman friend and her social worker.

The event was held over two evenings; much information was given to the Conference participants to prepare them for the many decisions they would need to make. During the meetings, Joanna sent three powerful letters from outside the room for her representative to read to the Conference participants. In the first letter she directly challenged Robert, the offender, saying that he was not taking enough responsibility for what happened. As a result, Robert apologized and took full responsibility. In the second letter she stated that she did not want Robert to lose his job so that he could pay for the self-defense lessons she wanted to take. In the third letter she expressed her concern that she not run into him while she was in the early stages of her recovery. She stated that she did not want him to come to the area where she lived and visited, including where she socialized on Friday and Saturday nights, even if he was under escort.

The Conference worked out a plan that met all of Joanna's requests. Robert would not lose his job, but he was not allowed to leave his place of work for any reason unless under escort. He was to be transported to and from his place of work each day. The plan required him to be under 24-hour supervision until he had completed a program for sexual offenders. All the conditions Joanna asked for, including 24-hour supervision, were to be made conditions of bail for a minimum of six months. This meant that Robert could be arrested immediately if found in breach of his bail. The plan called for Robert to be placed under the guardianship of the Director General of Social Welfare until he was 19. In turn, the police agreed that the charges could be amended to be an unlawful sexual connection, a lesser charge.

In short, the Conference developed a plan that met the needs of the victim and placed the offender into an extended program to minimize the immediate and long-term risks to the community. The offender would be held accountable, and his legal expenses were minimized.

On the day following the event, I phoned the caregiver to see how Joanna was coping in the aftermath. The caregiver said, "It's absolutely amazing. When we got home last night, Joanna walked in the door and said, 'I don't need to wear this coat anymore.' She slipped it off her shoulders and let it drop to the floor." Joanna had worn the coat ever since she was abused. The day after the Conference met, "She was present in a different way than I had ever seen her before. She looked as if an incredible weight had been lifted from her, and she was full of smiles and energy."

Robert completed all his obligations, including giving the police a DNA sample and paying for Joanna's self-defense classes. He stayed under supervision and finished the long-term plan under the care and protection status within the guardianship of Social Welfare. He faced the fact that he did not have the right to victimize others, while acknowledging that he needed help to live successfully and positively within the community.

This plan pushed boundaries: typically the boy would have gone to jail. And that would likely have led to his committing further offenses, eventually destroying any hope of his living successfully within the community. The potential outcome of this case was so ground-breaking that the police were not willing to shoulder responsibility for it alone. They wanted a judge to take that responsibility. The judge agreed, and she was given no cause for regret.

At the end of the first six months Robert was discharged from the Youth Court because he had successfully completed his agreement. Joanna, although only 13 years old, was a very strong person who used the Conference to meet her own needs for healing.

Through this case, I learned that even very young victims need to have a voice, that over-protection can be disempowering. A young person like Joanna can know what she needs for her own well-being and can initiate healing through the Conference process.

Allan and Howard: About this book

Family Group Conferences like this one are the primary forum in New Zealand for dealing with serious youth crime, as well as child welfare issues. This book is about this decision-making process in the youth justice arena, the Conferences (known as "FGCs") themselves, but also the juvenile justice system that is built around these Conferences.

Since their introduction in New Zealand in 1989, Family Group Conferences (sometimes with other names such as "community group conferences" or "community accountability conferences") have been adopted and adapted in many places throughout the world. They have been used as decision-making processes in many arenas, including child welfare, school discipline, and criminal justice, both juvenile and adult. In fact, Family Group Conferences have emerged as one of the most promising models of restorative justice.

There are, however, several different forms of FGCs. The most widely known model is based on an Australian adaptation; this model has strongly influenced the approach used by the Thames Valley Police in the United Kingdom, the Royal Canadian Mounted Police, and that of many communities in North America. New Zealand's method has some distinctive and important features that deserve consideration. It is the original model and the source of the term "Family Group Conference."

This *Little Book of Family Group Conferences* is designed to provide an introduction to FGCs, New Zealand style. We will describe the overall approach and provide information about how an FGC is conducted. Although this is not a complete how-to manual, it does provide many of the basics, especially when used in conjunction with other restorative justice material such as *The Little Book of Restorative Justice* or other material like that listed in the Appendices. And while some of the information is specific to New Zealand, much about the approach can be and has been adapted to many other settings.

Having said that, we do want to caution against simple replication of the model. New Zealand's FGCs are deliberately designed to allow individual Conferences to be adjusted to the cultures of those who participate. Nevertheless, no model should simply be copied and plugged into another context. We urge you to take from this what fits, to adapt it as necessary to your own setting. In doing so, however, we emphasize the importance of dialogue, of listening to each other, especially to the "stakeholders" (those most impacted by the crime), and to indigenous and minority groups in your community. Moreover, we cannot emphasize enough the importance of grounding practice in principle. We suggest the concept of restorative justice as a starting point for a discussion of principles.

A few words, yet, about the authors of this book. Allan MacRae is currently the Manager of Coordinators for the Southern Region of New Zealand, overseeing Family Group Conferences for both Youth Justice, and Care and Protection. Prior to taking this position, he was Youth Justice Coordinator for the capital city of Wellington. This *Little Book* draws upon and systematizes his experience there. When the pronoun "I" is used it refers to Allan.

Co-author Howard Zehr, Co-Director of the Conflict Transformation Program at Eastern Mennonite University (Harrisonburg, Virginia), is considered one of the founders of the field of restorative justice and is often called upon to interpret restorative justice in various parts of the world. He has frequently lectured and consulted in New Zealand.

Over a number of years of teaching together, visiting each other, and fishing together, we—Allan and Howard—have become friends. By combining our perspectives and talents, we hope to translate the practice of FGCs into a form that will be helpful to you.

2.
An Overview

During the 1980s, New Zealand faced a crisis familiar to other western nations around the world. Thousands of children, especially members of minority groups, were being removed from their homes and placed in foster care or institutions. The juvenile justice system was overburdened and ineffective. New Zealand's incarceration rate for young people was one of the highest in the world, but its crime rate also remained high. At the same time, New Zealand's punitive approach was also in part a "welfare" model. Although young people were being punished, they were also being rewarded by receiving attention. Yet they were not being required to address the actual harm they had caused.

Especially affected was the minority Maori population, the indigenous people of New Zealand. Maori leaders pointed out that the western system of justice was a foreign imposition. In their cultural tradition, judges did not mete out punishment. Instead, the whole community was involved in the process, and the intended outcome was repair. Instead of focusing on blame, they wanted to know "why," because they argued that finding the cause of crime is part of resolving it. Instead of punishment ("Let shame be the punishment" is a Maori proverb), they were concerned with healing and prob-lem-solving. The Maori also pointed out that the West-ern system, which undermined the family and dispro-portionately incarcerated Maori youth, emerged from a larger pattern of institutional racism. They argued per-suasively that cultural identity is based on three prima-ry institutional pillars—law, religion, and education—and when any of these undermines or ignores the values and traditions of the indigenous people, a system of racism is operating.

Because of these concerns, in the late 1980s the gov-ernment initiated a process of listening to communities throughout the country. Through this listening process, the Maori recommended that the resources of the extended family and the community be the source of any effort to address these is-sues. The FGC process emerged as the central tool to do this in the child protection and youth justice systems.

FGCs are intended to empower and value participants, while building upon the resources of the extended family and community.

In 1989 the legislature passed a landmark Act of Parliament. The Children, Young Persons and Their Families Act totally revamped the focus and process of juvenile jus-tice in New Zealand. Although it did not use this termi-nology until later, the New Zealand legal system became the first in the world to institutionalize a form of restora-tive justice. Family Group Conferences became the hub of New Zealand's entire juvenile justice system. In New Zealand today, an FGC, not a courtroom, is intended to be the normal site for making such decisions.

The Conference

FGCs are a kind of decision-making meeting, a face-to-face encounter involving offenders and their families, victims and their supporters, a police representative, and others. Organized and led by a Youth Justice Coordinator, a facilitator who is a social services professional, this approach is designed to support offenders as they take responsibility and change their behavior, to empower the offenders' families to play an important role in this process, and to address the victims' needs. Unlike restorative justice programs attached to justice systems elsewhere, this group together formulates the *entire outcome* or disposition, not just restitution. Importantly— and remarkably—they do this by *consensus* of all the participants, not by a mere majority or the decree of an official. Victim, offender, family members, youth advocate, or police can individually block an outcome if one of them is unsatisfied.

Particular Characteristics of New Zealand FGCs

- **intended for serious offenses**
- **the hub of the entire system**
- **governed by principles**
- **deals with the entire outcome**
- **uses consensus decision-making**
- **family-centered**
- **offers a family caucus**
- **aims at cultural adaptability and appropriateness**

Although there are similar elements in most Conferences, FGCs are intended to be adapted to the needs and perspectives of the participants. One of the goals of the process is to be *culturally appropriate,* and another is that it should *empower families.* It is the job of the coordinator to help the families determine who should be present and to design a process that will be appropriate for the needs and traditions of those involved.

Thus, there is not a scripted model in which the facilitator follows a predetermined text. While there is often a common overall pattern to Conferences, each is to be adapted to the situation. An element common to most Conferences, however, is a family caucus sometime during the event. Here the offender and family are left alone to discuss what has happened and to develop a proposal to bring back to the victim and the rest of the Conference.

Like the facilitator in other forms of restorative justice encounters, the coordinator of an FGC must seek to be impartial, balancing the concerns and interests of all parties. However, he or she is charged with making sure a plan is developed that addresses causes as well as reparation, that holds the offender adequately accountable, and that is realistic. The facilitator also must make sure that the Conference addresses issues of follow-up and monitoring. Who is to do what and when, and who is to monitor this, are all part of the plan that emerges from an FGC.

The system

In New Zealand, Family Group Conferences are not only a kind of meeting or encounter, they are the hub of an entire youth justice system.

Most countries and communities which employ restorative justice programs—FGCs or otherwise—use such programs or Conferences on a case-by-case basis, at the discretion of the legal system. The courtroom is the norm, and restorative justice is an add-on or diversion from it. In New Zealand, however, the Family Group Conference is the norm, and the courtroom is the backup.

An FGC is both a Conference and a justice system.

The system is designed so that all of the more serious juvenile cases are to be referred to an FGC, with the exception of murder and manslaughter. In New Zealand, a special branch of the police—Youth Aid Officers—are designated to work with young people. They work at prevention and law enforcement, but also serve as the prosecution, deciding what charges to file or "lay." This is why these officers must be present at an FGC, since the FGC will together decide what charges will ultimately be filed, or whether all charges should be dropped. The police have a significant role in deciding whether a case will go to an FGC or will be disposed of without such a Conference.

More minor offenses—about 80% of juvenile crimes that come to the attention of the police—are intended to be handled by the police through "cautioning" and release (in the U.S., these are sometimes called "reprimand and release"), or through diversionary approaches such as informal victim-offender mediation.

When an accused young person denies a charge but it is proven in Court, the case must go back to an FGC who will recommend to the Court how the proven charge should be addressed. Even though a Conference would not be held to address murder or manslaughter charges, a Conference may still be required to address custody issues while the offender awaits trial or sentencing. The Conference would consider alternatives to custody, or what should be provided to the young person while in custody, such as cultural, religious, or other needs or wishes of the family. This Conference could also recommend who is allowed to visit the young person while in custody.

New Zealand law identifies four types of youth justice Family Group Conferences. **"Custody Conferences"** must be held when a young person is placed in custody after denying the charge. **"Charge Proven Conferences"** are called for by a court when a young person has denied guilt but is then found guilty in court. **"Intention to Charge Conferences"** (the young person is not arrested, but is referred directly to a Youth Justice Coordinator for a Conference) decide if a child or young person should be prosecuted, or how the matter can be dealt with in another way. **"Charge Not Denied Conferences"** (the young person is arrested and brought before the court) are directed by the court (as soon as the young person admits responsibility for what has occurred) to recommend one of the following—the charges should be removed from court; a plan for addressing the charges; amendments to the charges; how the court should dispose of the matter.

Most FGCs, then, are not intended to involve courts significantly. Only when Conferences are held to make sentence recommendations, or when a Conference recommends some court monitoring or enforcement, is there to be oversight by the court. On occasion, a court-ordered Conference recommends that the charges be withdrawn from the court to promote less formal monitoring. This can only happen when the police agree,

Youth Justice Process

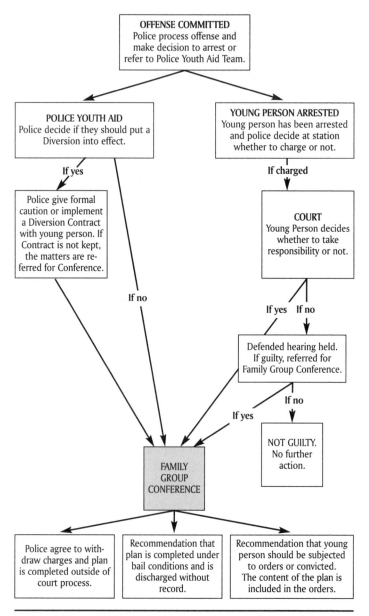

when the police and other Conference participants have confidence that the plan will be completed, and when the perpetrator shows genuine remorse.

Judge Fred McElrea, a prominent New Zealand judge and advocate of restorative justice, argues that this approach appropriately makes the community, not the court, the center of decision-making. Not only has the number of young people appearing in court in New Zealand dropped, but less court time is needed to deal with them. Consequently, the court can focus on safe-guarding the process and dealing with special cases.

On page 16 is a simplified flowchart providing an overview of the process or system.

3.
Principled Practice

The cornerstone of the youth justice system in New Zealand is the Family Group Conference. The system works because all elements, from the police through the courts, are guided by principles and goals established in the 1989 Act. There are numerous examples of practitioners straying from these principles and goals. But if they are followed—if the goals and principles are regularly used in designing and running Conferences—they will lead to restorative practice. *In our opinion, these clear goals and principles, and cultivated habits of referring to them in making decisions, will result in good practice and, ultimately, a restorative approach.*

Seven goals

The seven primary goals of youth justice in New Zealand can be summarized like this:

- **Diversion**—A key goal is to keep young people out of the courts and to prevent labeling them as offenders. Underlying this are several assumptions: a) contact with the criminal justice system often increases, rather than decreases, offending; b) most youthful offending is developmental rather than pathological, so most offenders will grow out of it;

and c) community-based sanctions can focus better on needs and behaviors than custodial ones can.

- **Accountability**—Offenders must be held accountable and thus encouraged to accept responsibility for their actions and to repair the harm they have caused. This concept is explored further in the principles below.

- **Involving the victim**—Victims' needs must be addressed, and victims themselves must have an opportunity to be part of deciding the outcomes. Victim involvement also provides genuine accountability for offenders.

- **Involving and strengthening the offender's family**—The offender's family should be involved in the processes and outcomes. It is needed to encourage its young person to make good decisions and to provide the resources to carry them out. An important underlying assumption is that families, even fragmented or dysfunctional ones, are able to help their young people work through the effects of their behavior if they give them support.

- **Consensus decision-making**—Outcomes should be agreed upon by all participants, not imposed by a majority or "from above."

- **Cultural appropriateness**—Processes and assistance should be adapted to the cultural perspectives and needs of the participants.

- **Due process**—The young person's rights must be respected. Specialized "youth advocates" are appointed to assist in the process and to watch that these rights are observed.

Seven guiding principles

To achieve these goals, the 1989 Act spells out seven guiding principles for the Family Group Conference process in youth justice cases. These principles apply not only to the FGC process, but to all youth justice procedures in New Zealand.

- *Criminal proceedings should be avoided unless the public interest requires otherwise.* The system, including FGCs, does need to consider public interest.

  In practice, this means that the coordinator needs to come to the FGC with the information needed to consider alternatives. The presence of a police representative ensures that public interest factors are not overlooked.

- *Criminal justice processes should not be used to provide assistance.* Criminal proceedings should not be used to address welfare needs such as protection, residence, or care.

  Prior to the 1989 Act, the "welfare approach" had often used criminal proceedings to try to meet the welfare needs of young people. This resulted in unnecessary charges and increased rates of institutionalization.

- *Families should be strengthened.* The Act specifies that any measures taken should be designed to: 1) strengthen the family group; and 2) foster the ability of the family to develop its own means of dealing with offending within the family.

  Most parents of misbehaving children feel helpless. Parents are often confused about their options and the resources available to help. Typical justice responses, which commonly shift matters from parents to professionals, increase the parents' sense of helplessness and frustration. Justice responses, then, should be designed to help the family deal with its own problems.

When an FGC is convened, it is important to ensure that the assailant's family has the appropriate networks to allow the FGC plan to succeed. The first preference is to enlist the support of extended family, but, where this is not available or sufficient, creating a community of support around the family is the next best option.

The Act assumes—and subsequent experience confirms—that when families are encouraged to "put things right" with the victim(s) and community, and given support to do so, the results are more effective. When the family develops its own plans for reparation, its members have greater ownership and commitment to make the FGC reparation plan work. An additional advantage of the FGC process is that youth offenders' siblings witness the modeling of accountability, responsibility, and reparation. This is a form of prevention.

- *Children should be kept in the community if at all possible.* Research has shown that young offenders feel isolated within their communities. In Wellington, the capital city of New Zealand, most youth who offend are Samoans and Maori who live outside their tribal areas or Caucasians who have been separated from their support networks by a family split or an employment relocation by their parents.

  Removing youths from their natural communities only adds to their feeling of not belonging, which can lead to their losing respect for their current communities. If youths do not respect or feel unjustly treated by their communities, if they do not feel they belong, it is easier for them to offend against them.

Young people who were raised outside a family environment have little experience on which to base their own parenting skills. Those who have had extended periods in residential or institutional care also lack the skills to socialize and to develop support networks within their communities. Gangs and subcultures pick them up. In fact, incarceration contributes to the problem by making many youths feel angry towards society, creating within them a strong feeling of not belonging and preventing them from developing the very skills they need for positive change.

- *The child or young person's age must be taken into account.* Youth are still developing, and decision-makers should remember that a young person's behavior and needs are profoundly affected by this process. Except for murder and manslaughter, young people under the age of 17 normally go to an FGC, not a court, where decisions are made about their overall needs and responsibilities.

- *Personal development should be promoted using the least restrictive option.* This principle, which overlaps with those above, says that: 1) any sanctions should be designed to promote the development of the young person within his or her family group; and 2) within those circumstances, the least restrictive form that is appropriate should be taken. One of the reasons for this principle is that children and youth have a strong sense of justice. Overly restrictive responses offend that sense of justice, which every community should be enhancing in its youth.

- *The interests of victims must be considered.* This principle reminds practitioners that victims are an essential part of the equation. Justice must provide an opportunity for victims to be involved, to help define their own needs, and to have their needs addressed.

The "interests of victims" principle exists for the sake of victims, but also for the sake of offenders. It is very effective to have young people focus on the impact of their actions. They gain a clear understanding of what they have done and how they can correct the impact to the best of their abilities. Unlike punishment, this is true accountability since it has natural and logical consequences.

In processes where the offender is held accountable to *the state,* s/he has very little connection to

Seven Goals	**Seven Principles**
• diversion • accountability • victim involvement • family empowerment • consensus decision-making • cultural appropriateness • due process	• avoid criminal proceedings • don't use justice for assistance • strengthen families • keep offenders in community • take age into account • use least restrictive option • consider victim interests

the offense, the victim, the family, or the community where the offense occurred. Any punitive consequence for the offense is viewed by the youth as an act of vengeance by the community and further contributes to her/his isolation. This does not help the offender understand the real impact of what s/he has done.

The Family Group Conference places priority on the victim's needs, which may include financial settlement as partial reparation. The FGC gives the victim a voice, and this can be healing to both the victim and the youth who has offended. When young persons complete their commitments to the victims, they often feel better about themselves. This in turn contributes toward a more positive lifestyle. Recidivism research suggests that offenders who have put things right are less likely to re-offend. So when youth are held accountable in a restorative manner, there is a greater chance of a satisfactory outcome for victims, for offenders, and for the community.

Since 1989, the practice of FGCs in New Zealand has varied in quality. In some areas the approach has been highly successful. Where it has not lived up to its potential, we believe it is because of a failure to use and follow these principles and goals consistently. Where the Youth Justice system has been successful, these principles and goals have been used not only to shape policy, but also to guide decisions in each case and each situation.

Again, we point to the importance of goals and principles for guiding good practice. Although standards of practice and ethical guidelines can be helpful, we suggest that clear principles and goals are even more important.

We strongly encourage any community that is designing restorative or conflict-resolution processes to establish appropriate goals and principles. Having done that, be sure to draw on culturally-appropriate values as you use those goals and principles as a guide to practice.

4.
Organizing a Family Group Conference

New Zealand law establishes different kinds of Family Group Conferences for child offenders and youth offenders. FGCs held for child offenders (between 10 and 14 years old) primarily focus on the welfare and interests of the child more than on the offending behavior as such. Here the well-being of the child is paramount, but that is, of course, coupled with obligations to teach the child accountability and responsibility. Youth offenders (those between 14 and 17 years old), on the other hand, can be held criminally accountable. Regardless of the type, the basic shape of the FGC process is the same. The following is a description of the roles involved and how a Conference is put together and conducted.

The Coordinator's role

The person who organizes and oversees the overall process, and normally facilitates the Conference itself, is called a Youth Justice Coordinator.

The Coordinator receives reports from the police and

meets with them to explore alternatives to filing criminal charges. Indeed, collaboration with the police is a key element in communities where the Youth Justice system has been especially effective in reducing crime. In fact, in an effort to increase collaboration, a recent focus in New Zealand is on creating "youth offending teams" which comprise all of the professionals involved in Youth Justice.

Once it has been decided to take a case to an FGC, the Coordinator's tasks are to:

1) prepare the parties,
2) convene and facilitate the Conference,
3) monitor the principles of the Act,
4) record the agreements or plans, and
5) communicate the results to the appropriate people and agencies.

More specifically, the Coordinator is required to:

a. Consult with the offender and the *family* of the offender about:
  - the process to be used in the FGC, and the date, time, and venue for the FGC and,
  - who should be invited. Under New Zealand law, the offender's extended family members are entitled to attend the FGC, so it is important to consult with the family about what additional support they may require.

b. Consult with the *victim* about:
  - whether s/he wishes to attend and, if so, the date, time, and venue for the FGC, and,
  - his/her rights in the process. This includes the different ways in which s/he can participate in the process. Victims may send a representative, have phone contact with the FGC, write letters,

or have the FGC Coordinator put information through to the FGC on his/her behalf. This information may be presented as a video or audio tape or simply be conveyed as a verbal message. If the victim or a representative does attend, that person is entitled to have support people come along. The victim may decline to participate at all. Good support for victims encourages them to attend and to receive benefit from the Conference. Research shows that the best results are achieved when victims attend, but it must be their choice to do so.

c. Take all reasonable steps to give notification, including date, time, and venue, of the Family Group Conference to all those who are entitled to attend.

d. Find out the views of those persons who are involved but are unable to attend the Family Group Conference.

e. Ensure that relevant information and advice is made available to the Family Group Conference that will enable the FGC to carry out its functions. This includes providing information about services and networks in the community that may be relevant. The Coordinator needs to have a well-functioning network within the community and with other professionals.

f. Convene and guide the Conference itself, adapting it to the cultural setting and to the needs of the parties.

g. Ensure that the decisions, recommendations, and plans which emerge are within the principles that guide the process.

h. Record the decisions, recommendations, or plans made by the Family Group Conference and ensure that they are made available to the appropriate persons and agencies (such as the police and court). If the plans require the service of an agency or a person who is not present at the FGC, the Coordinator must seek that entity's agreement after the FGC.

i. Reconvene the FGC if two people who attended the FGC request it, the plan calls for it, the Court orders it, or if the Coordinator or police feel there is a need to reconvene the FGC (e.g., if parts are not working).

As a facilitator, the Coordinator's role includes something similar to mediation. As the multiple task list above suggests, however, the term "mediation" is not totally appropriate. Like a mediator, the Coordinator must seek to be impartial and balanced and may not impose outcomes or solutions. However, the Coordinator is responsible for helping the police or courts make decisions about the process, ensuring that the offender is held adequately accountable during the Conference, and seeing that the plan adopted by the FGC is manageable, appropriate, and monitored. In short, the Coordinator is mandated to ensure that the process and outcomes are guided by the principles.

Conference participants

In addition to the Coordinator, the Youth Justice System in New Zealand makes provision for the following participants in an FGC. However, attendance is only mandated for offenders, family members of the offenders, and police representatives.

- *Offenders and their families,* including extended family,

- *Victims or victim representatives,* and supporters,

- *Police representatives* (Youth Aid Officer),

- *Youth Advocates.* Special lawyers are carefully selected and appointed to assist in Youth Justice cases. They are to safeguard the rights of the young offenders and assist the process; their role is not adversarial.

- *Lay Advocates.* These may be appointed to advise on cultural matters, to help make sure the process is culturally appropriate for those involved.

- *Social workers* can attend if the young offender's family wishes, or if the agency has legal custody, guardianship, or supervision, or if it is required to give support to the child/young person.

- *Information-givers.* In some cases, someone with special information (e.g., community, school, or church representatives) may attend, but only for the relevant part of the Conference.

- Other *care-givers,* i.e., any person currently having care of the offending child or young person.

Preparation

Let's assume that you are a Youth Justice Coordinator charged with putting together an FGC, New Zealand style.

Begin the process by sending letters to the victims, the offender, and the offender's parents. These letters should include a pamphlet explaining the process and should ask the recipients to contact the Coordinator within 72 hours. Use the written word only to open the opportunity to communicate or to confirm an agreement that has been reached.

If you have not heard from recipients of the letters within a few days (in New Zealand, short statutory time limits of two to three weeks are placed on the process), follow up with a phone call. On the phone, ask to meet with them to explain their rights and options in more detail. Most people agree to a meeting in their home. Here are some observations and suggestions growing out of our experience as practitioners:

• Person-to-person communications are more likely to build rapport and understanding than phone or letter contact. When you communicate in this way you receive the benefit of full interaction. Real communication includes listening to the tone of someone's voice and a visual observation of body language. For example, people may say they will attend the FGC, especially the victim or the victim's associates, but their body language tells you they are not feeling comfortable with that decision. By acknowledging their apparent discomfort, you can open a discussion about their level of comfort and address the issues that cause it. Experience has shown that unless the discomfort is addressed, people usually decide at the last minute not to attend.

• The next best form of communication is by phone. It is important, though, to try first to meet the victim or associate face-to-face. Experience shows that the percentage of Conferences with victims attending is significantly higher when victims are invited in person. So even if victims may express on the phone that they do not wish to attend the FGC, ask if they would be willing to meet with you so you can explain their rights in the FGC process. Most agree to

> ## Victims may
>
> - attend all or part,
> - decline to participate,
> - send representatives,
> - send information.

meet with the Coordinator, and then end up attending the Conference.

- The written word is the most unreliable form of communication. Letters and emails are often misunderstood. Do not rely on letters or email as a sole form of communication.
- Good communications skills are required by anyone facilitating a Family Group Conference process. The facilitator needs to be able to explain the process, negotiate and seek agreements, guide the meetings, and record the decisions accurately. The facilitator's communication skills need to function well in a number of situations, including the FGC, meetings with the enforcement agencies, and the court.

Working with victims

The initial reason for meeting with victims is to inform them of their rights and to give them information about the process. Although it is preferable to have them at the Conference, and usually beneficial to them, it is inappropriate to pressure them into attending.

In New Zealand, victims have the right to participate in three ways. First, they have the right to be present and to bring support people with them. This could be a family member, close friend, caregiver, or a representative of a victim support organization. Second, they may send a representative, and that person may bring support people. Third, victims may choose to send information only. In this third option, however, they do not have a right to object to or disagree with the outcome of the Conference, although they can refuse any outcome that involves them directly. This could include a personal apology or work done by the offender for them.

You should first consult with the victims on the date, time, and venue for the Conference. Because the victims are being asked to give their time to attend an FGC, share information that may help them decide the value of giving that time. Often victims fear re-victimization, and it is helpful to be able to tell them that the Conference process is designed to safeguard against this. Other factors to share are the successes that are being achieved through the FGC process. Some examples of these achievements are in the Appendices (pages 67-70).

The majority of victims choose to attend, but some require assistance, like travel, babysitters, or compensation for the loss of income. The New Zealand system normally provides some financial assistance for such needs. To accommodate work schedules, FGCs are often held in the evenings.

Again, it is important for you as Coordinator to be flexible about how victims wish to be involved, to support their needs, and to ensure that they choose how they want to participate. Present all the options with as much information as possible so victims can make an educated decision that best suits them. Whether victims choose to be involved or not, it is important that victims' interests be taken into account in Conference plans.

There are a number of ways that a victim can participate without actually being in the Conference. The Coordinator may share information on the victim's behalf or the victim can choose to send a video or audio message to be played during the Conference. A victim may participate by phone for whole or part of the Conference or can choose to observe the Conference through a closed-circuit video link and be supported in another room by a social worker and other persons. Notes written by the victim can be read to the offender and the Conference as a whole. All of these ways help to insure that the victim's wishes are included in the plan.

Victims or their representatives should know that they have a choice as to whether to participate in the full Conference or only in part of it. The latter usually means the victim will attend the information-sharing part of the Conference. (That usually precedes the private deliberations between the offender and his/her family.)

In most cases, if the victim is not going to remain for the full Conference, the offender's family gives the victim assurance that they will include the victim's wishes in the final plan, and the Coordinator agrees to monitor this.

Victims may also choose to become involved at a planned reconvening of the FGC, when the offending child or youth has demonstrated some commitment and taken steps to " put things right."

In some cases, such as traffic offenses or drug charges, there is no identifiable victim. In these cases the community is considered the victim, and police represent the community. However, it would be possible to involve surrogate victims as information-givers, such as those who have suffered from drunk driving or drug use. But it must be remembered that they cannot be there as entitled participants, nor do they have the right to remain for the whole Conference, or to agree or disagree with the plan. There is the risk that they may expect the young person to put right what happened to them.

As Coordinator, you should explain the process to the victim, as well as the fact that you are consulting with the offender and the offender's family. Since New Zealand law allows and encourages the offender and family to take responsibility for shaping the process, you may need to check back with the victim about special process requests the offender may make. If there are cultural differences, you may need to negotiate between the parties about such things as the use of prayers, as discussed below.

You should also inform victims that they are entitled to tell the offender how angry they are and how the offense has affected them. They may ask questions as well. Make clear that they should not agree to the plan which will outline how the young person will be held accountable unless they feel it is fair and just. Explain that the FGC is not about debating the offender's guilt with the victim, since the FGC can only make decisions affecting the child or young person if the charge is admitted or proven in court.

When working with victims, offenders, and their families, it is important to ask whether they wish to start the Conference with a prayer or blessing, or whether there are other cultural protocols they would like to have incorporated. For many Maori, South Pacific, and other regional groups, a prayer is culturally very important. Encourage them to say a prayer if they wish to do so and to use their customary language and traditions. It is the Coordinator's responsibility to inform both "sides"—victims as well as offenders—of these wishes so they know what to expect. You may need to do some back-and-forth communication between victim and offender families to determine a process that is appropriate for both. You may also need to provide translators for either or both parties.

Working with offender and family

The first piece of conflict resolution work is facilitating the convening of the Conference (date, time, venue, who will attend) and ensuring that victims' interests are looked after in the process the Conference will follow. The Coordinator is required to consult with the offending child/young person's family about those same details and the process the FCG will follow.

It is important early on to check the offender's—and his/her family's—understanding of the charge. If there are discrepancies or misunderstandings, ask the police and the youth's advocate (lawyer) to clarify them.

Because many families are entering the process for the first time, explain that the law entitles them to have private deliberation time (the family caucus) and that the family's deliberations usually divide the Conference into three main parts or phases (as explained later in this chapter).

Advise the offender's family that their decision-making is critical because the FGC gives a clear priority to young offenders who are held accountable within the support of their extended families. The FGC process should enable their best decision-making.

Once the family has an understanding of the FGC process and of their own responsibilities, ask for a list of people they would like to invite as support. It is important to clarify that "family" is to be broadly interpreted and should include anyone who can assist in putting a plan together or in helping to resource it.

Often the child/young person has someone s/he looks up to. If so, that person should be included in the FGC. A young offender can be greatly encouraged by having someone s/he respects helping to put things right, and to do so with a positive attitude. This person can also act as an advocate for the child/young person because an offense often puts a strain on the child/young person's relationship with his/her family. This is especially true when a family member is the victim, e.g., an assault on a parent. Advise the family that other adults who are outside the family, but have a positive relationship with their child/young person, may also be of assistance; perhaps a team coach, youth group leader, minister, or teacher.

If the family does not have extended networks, it is important to assist them in developing such support. For this purpose, the Coordinator needs to be well connected in the community. Coordinators ought to create working relationships with a number of organizations from different cultures and with different resources. These organizations can offer venues and support for families. It is not uncommon for these organizations also to be contracted to monitor an outcome or the total plan.

For a number of reasons, the offender's family may not have extended family or adequate resources to meet the obligations that a Family Group Conference requires. An example of this was a refugee family that had no extended family within New Zealand; the victim of the assault was one of the offender's caregivers. An arrangement was made with two migrant and refugee organizations to support the family.

When you visit the family in their home before the FGC, offer to put them in contact with one or more organizations that may be able to help them. This would include the opportunity for them to meet with the organization's representatives before the family decides whether or not to involve them in the FGC.

For a very serious charge, the plan may require high levels of supervision; spreading the burden can make the difference between success and failure. A failure may not be the fault of the young person, but rather the adult's lack of endurance in carrying out the supervision. Having other organizations and networks involved along with the family can make a great difference in the plan's succeeding.

Once the FGC is arranged, invitation letters should be sent out to all identified participants.

The Conference

Again, Family Group Conferences can take many forms, depending on the culture and/or religion of the participants. What is outlined in this section should only be used as a guide.

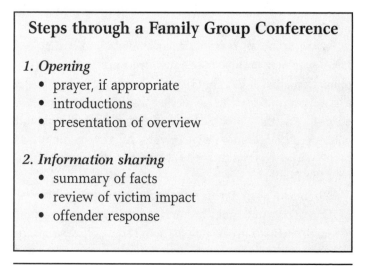

Steps through a Family Group Conference

1. Opening
- prayer, if appropriate
- introductions
- presentation of overview

2. Information sharing
- summary of facts
- review of victim impact
- offender response

- information about forming the plan
- refreshments (optional)

3. Family deliberations

4. Reaching agreement
- proposal
- negotiation
- finalization of plan

5. Closing
- prayer, if appropriate

Setting up the meeting room

Make sure that the room has adequate resources for the Conference. Space and seating are the most critical. Try to allow for more seating and space than may be required. This allows for more flexibility of choice by the participants.

Sometimes victims and their supporters might like to leave a seat or two between themselves and the offender's family. There will also be times when the offender's family feels uncomfortable sitting together; family dynamics may cause them to want space between them (e.g., the parents may be separated).

The seating arrangement may change during the course of the FGC as participants' comfort levels increase. For example, the offender may feel uncomfortable being with his/her family at the beginning of the FGC but may choose to sit with them by the conclusion of the FGC.

It is very important that the venue is free of interruption from unexpected visitors and phone calls. This can be a problem particularly if it is decided that the FGC will be held at a family's home. When this option is chosen, contract with the family to unplug the phone.

Other resources that are required include access to another room to facilitate private deliberations, and having pens and writing material in both rooms. It is also important to provide culturally-appropriate refreshments. Some participants may want to bring their own food to contribute since sharing food with the others may be an important part of their culture.

When laying out the seating, remember that a circle or horseshoe shape is often most appropriate, both culturally and to enhance communication. Discourage participants from sitting outside the circle. The seating arrangement should allow people to leave the room with a minimum of inconvenience and without having to walk past a person with whom they are in conflict.

Phase 1. Opening the Conference

As participants arrive, ask them to sit where they feel comfortable, but within the seating set up for the FGC.

If the family has indicated that they would like the FGC to start with a *blessing or prayer,* begin with that, offered by a member of the family or a support person. Often in New Zealand the blessing or prayer is said in the family's first language and in a way that is appropriate to their religion or culture. This is very important because it demonstrates your respect for the family's values. A member of the family can translate if the prayer is not in a language understood by all. On rare occasions the Coordinator may be asked to say a blessing or prayer on behalf of the FGC.

The next step is to start the *introductions;* this is the first step if there is no blessing or prayer. Lead the introductions by introducing yourself by your name and your official position. State that it is the Coordinator's responsibility to facilitate the Family Group Conference and to explain the process for the FGC after the introductions. Then ask the other participants to introduce themselves, starting from the Coordinator's left. (Many, but not all, cultures follow a clockwise direction in meetings that are set in a circle or horseshoe.)

Ask the participants to include in their introductions the reasons that they are there. Getting participants to introduce themselves helps start their involvement in the process better than if you introduce them to one another.

Once the introductions have been completed, *outline the legal standing of the FGC and the process* for *this particular FGC*. Remind the participants that there is flexibility, and that if they need private time or a break they only need to indicate to the Coordinator that they would like that opportunity. Also, make it very clear that it is the Coordinator's responsibility to make sure the principles that guide the Youth Justice process are not compromised in the FGC or through the agreed outcomes. After explaining the principles and process, ask if there are any questions.

It is important to give the participants good information on what they are about to undertake, but most of this should have been given to the key participants prior to the FGC. An overview at the start of the Family Group Conference should last only about five minutes.

Phase 2: Information sharing

Now the focus shifts to the offending behavior or act. In most cases this would start with the *reading of the summary* of facts by the police. This summary sets out the facts on which the charges, or intended charges, are based. If the charges are denied, the FGC can go no further because the matter needs to be forwarded or returned to court for a defended hearing. Family Group Conferences can only make decisions or recommendations on charges that are admitted or proven by the court. But if the young person is going to deny the charges, you would normally know this before you set up a Conference.

Next, ask the young person whether s/he understands the charges and what they mean; then ask whether s/he admits or denies the offense. Make it clear to the alleged offender before the FGC and during the explanation of the process that s/he should not admit any charge s/he is not sure s/he has committed.

After the child or young person has admitted the charge, ask the victim or victims *to explain the impact* the offenses have had on them. From the pre-Conference communication with the victim, the Coordinator will have an idea about what questions need to be asked to help bring out his/her story. Advise the victim that it is important for the young person to see his/her anger and hurt, if that is what s/he feels.

Often FGCs deal with a number of charges, which means that there could be more than one victim present, or that some victims may have chosen to attend while others have not. In this situation, the Coordinator needs to decide whether the information from the victims who have not attended should be stated at this time, or whether it is better to have the attending victims go first. Try to read the body language of the victims. If they are looking comfortable or give an impression that they want to have their say, always have them go first. If they are looking hesitant or unlikely to share their feelings, then offer the absent victims' information first, trying to project into the FGC their anger and hurt, so the victims present feel more comfortable sharing theirs.

After the victims have shared their stories, you may wish to summarize the impact. Then ask the child or young person to tell the victims why s/he committed the offenses. If necessary, help the young person share his/her information. When the young person is done, it may be helpful to summarize what s/he has said. You may also want to ask the offender how s/he feels about what s/he has heard, and perhaps even whether s/he has anything to say to the victim. However, you may also wish to wait and see what emerges from the family caucus.

This can be the point where the victims start asking *questions* of the child or young person. If this leads to a natural flowing communication between the victim and the offender, it is important for the Coordinator to reduce his or her facilitation.

The first objective when facilitating a FGC is to establish communication between the two parties. When that communication comes to a natural end, you may want to ask the offender's family to summarize how the offense has impacted them. Also ask the family to tell the FGC what they would like the FGC to hear about their child/young person's actions, any other statements they may wish to make, or questions they may wish to ask. It is critical to develop the communication between the victims and the offending young person and his/her family.

Youth advocates who attend FGCs know that their job is not adversarial and that they are there to be supportive, providing information or advice, but not interfering with the process. Before the offender's family moves into its private deliberation, you may wish to ask such professionals whether they have any further information they would like to give the offender's family.

Phase 3. Family caucus and deliberations

Once all the relevant information has been shared, prepare for family deliberations. The offender's family is entitled to have private deliberations and the Coordinator must offer it to them, although they may choose not to take it. Before this happens, though, it may help to summarize the harms and impacts, as well as the preventive issues, that the offender's family will need to address. It is important to provide the family with newsprint and markers to use in planning or presenting.

This is a time when most FGCs take a break for refreshments. Family deliberations often come more naturally when they follow or include refreshments.

As the Coordinator, be sure to observe what happens at this point. If the participants stay together, the healing has already started. If the victim and his/her support have prepared their refreshments and moved into the other room, it may indicate that they are still feeling uncomfortable. The most common reason for a victim to feel uncomfortable generally comes from a perceived lack of remorse from the offender.

It is wise to engage the victim in conversation by asking him/her how s/he feels about the FGC to this point. When there is a perceived lack of remorse, it is important to advise the victim that an offending child or young person is often unable to show his/her remorse until after the deliberations with his/her family, and explain why. The young person often enters the process with his/her own defense mechanisms well engaged, but after hearing the impact s/he has had on the victim and seeing the anger, and then talking with his/her own family, s/he is better able to let down his/her defenses.

The offender's family should be made aware that, if they wish, they can invite any of the FGC participants to come in to their deliberations to answer questions. This often occurs. Sometimes the family just wants to check that they are moving towards a plan that is going to be acceptable to the victim before they invest more time in it.

The family caucus provides an opportunity for:
- the offender and his/her family to discuss family matters and begin developing a plan;
- the victim and his/her supporters to talk about their needs and options with the coordinator, police, and other participants.

These family deliberations are a very critical part of the process for a number of reasons. First, the offender and his/her family have a chance to talk in private about the options and resources they have within the family. They may have been reluctant to put another family member on the spot in the larger forum. In private, they are able to investigate more personal issues like financial commitments, or personal requests for support from the extended family to cover resource needs, including time commitments that may be required to supervise parts of the plan.

Frequently, a family has to deal with issues within the family before they can focus on establishing a plan to address the offense. If the parents have separated, the incident can highlight the need for them to make new commitments about parenting or to decide with whom the young person will reside while s/he is held accountable for the offense. During the deliberations, the family may request that the Coordinator or another Conference participant join them for a short time to answer questions.

Victims often use this time to reflect with the police about what they would like to see in the plan and why. This is very positive, since the police feel more comfortable agreeing to a plan that meets the victims' needs. During this time, too, the victims are able to talk with their own support people and other Conference participants.

When the offender's family returns from their private deliberations, there is often a change of seating arrangements. For example, the youth may now sit with his or her family instead of sitting separately.

Phase 4. Reaching agreement

Offenders' families bring back quite varied suggestions. They may present a comprehensive plan, or a list of beginning ideas, or simply a statement that they have addressed only personal issues and now wish to put the plan together in the larger group. It is important not to make an initial judgment about what is presented at this point. Most often the family has an outline of a plan, but they want the larger group to assist them with the finer details.

Encourage the offending child/young person to present the plan. There are two main reasons for this. If the child/young person can present the plan, then the Coordinator can be reasonably comfortable that s/he understands it. Also, this tends to put the focus of the conversation back between the offender and the victim or victims.

After the young person has presented the plan that s/he and his/her family have developed, without interruption ask the victim what s/he would like to add or remove from the plan. Do this in a way that empowers the victim to feel s/he has a right to contribute to the plan. Avoid asking yes/no questions; don't ask the victim if s/he agrees or disagrees with the plan but encourage discussion on the plan with open-ended questions.

Once the victim has expressed his/her wishes and worked out the details with the offending young person and his/her family, it is time to involve the professionals (police and Youth Advocate). It is rare for the police representative to want an amendment that will take a victim's wish out of the plan, or something that has been offered to the victim. Rather, the police tend to focus on the public interest. When they know the victim's interests, the police are in a better position to weigh those alongside the community's interests.

The next step is not to ask for agreement on the plan, but to take more time to explore how the offender's family perceives the plan. Often a family member may express a wish that s/he is not sure how to implement. It is very important that the Coordinator does not make the decision, but offers a number of options from which the victim, as well as the offending young person and family, can choose. For example, a victim may say s/he would like to be kept informed of how the child/young person is progressing with the plan, but the young person is not sure how to meet this desire. The Coordinator can suggest that they consider a number of options with varying levels of interaction, ranging from a letter to the victim from the young person near the end of the plan, to reconvening the FGC to review progress.

Some joint activity to celebrate the successful completion of the plan is a way of bringing positive closure to a challenging situation for all involved. The offending young person's family may invite the victim to their home for a celebratory barbecue or meal. Such ideas provide additional motivation for the young person to complete the plan.

Once the plan is outlined, it is important to have a *reality check*. Go through the plan and make sure that

---

Core elements in a plan

- Putting things right for the victim (a priority).

- Returning something to the community.

- Addressing the underlying causes of the offending.

- Ensuring that the child/young person has the support s/he needs to meet his/her obligations.

---

each of the decisions is measurable and able to be monitored. Each decision needs to include a date by when it should be completed, who will insure that it is carried out, and what and how much needs to be undertaken. A community-work decision could read as follows:

Community Work

Robert will complete 40 hours of community work, with a minimum of five hours being completed per week. Robert's mother will arrange for this work to start within two weeks at the Salvation Army's home for the elderly. Verification will be through a letter from the Salvation Army recording the hours completed, which will be forwarded to the monitor of the plan.

Once all the outcomes have been made clear and measurable, ask the victim if s/he agrees with the total plan as presented. Then ask the offending young person's family if they agree; then seek the agreement of the police. If the victim is not present, let the participants know that you will contact the victim the next day to confirm that it meets with his/her needs or wishes.

It is important to ask the offending young person, "Do you believe you can complete this plan?" Explore any hesitancies with him/her. Even if s/he says yes, ask whether s/he feels that s/he is being set up to fail in any way. The aim is to ensure that the young person is not just saying yes to avoid the pressure of the moment. If his/her concern is opened up, more assistance can be provided to get him/her through the parts s/he views as being difficult. If the fear is about being home alone or having to keep a curfew, see if s/he could spend that time with another family member or a supportive friend.

When there is full agreement to the plan (which occurs in over 95% of FGCs), advise the offending young person to let the police, or social worker, or community representative, know if something beyond his/her control is preventing him/her from completing the plan.

When participants in a Conference cannot agree, there are two ways in which that outcome can be recorded. But first, let us state clearly that the negotiations within a Conference should be recorded "without prejudice." Therefore, if there is no agreement to any plan at all, the facilitator of the Conference should record only that the Conference could not reach agreement. Do not record the views of the different parties.

If, however, the participants do reach agreement on most parts of the plan, they could agree to record the

The plan in 4 parts

1. System issues

2. Reparation

3. Prevention

4. Monitoring

points on which they have agreement. Without noting the views or positions of the parties, the facilitator could record that agreement couldn't be reached on a specific point. For example, "The Conference was unable to make a recommendation on how the matter should be disposed, once the plan is completed," or "The Conference agreed that community work should be done but could not agree on the amount." This makes it clear to the court where some arbitration may be required.

Phase 5. Closing the Conference

If the meeting started with a blessing/prayer, then it usually should be closed with a blessing/prayer.

It is not uncommon for participants to remain and talk for a few minutes after the FGC has concluded, which clearly reflects the process's ability to bring people together who were separated by conflict. In many cases, victims offer offenders employment so they can pay off the reparation, but at a rate that still leaves the offender with money (e.g. a 50/50 split of his/her earnings until the reparation is paid in full).

In some cases, victims have had the offender socialize with them so the offender can find a new peer group or come to their home to make repairs. There is no limit on what can be put in a Family Group Conference plan under New Zealand law, with two exceptions: the maximum number of community work hours that can be ordered is 200, and court-ordered reparation is limited to actual loss and not to consequential or secondary loss.

The plan

The format of the plan is important. The best format is one that is clear and that groups the outcomes into the areas to which they apply. *All parts of the plan, including deadlines and expectations, should be spelled out clearly.*

Case example

In one Family Group Conference I facilitated, six organizations were represented. For the plan to succeed, they needed to work cooperatively together and ensure that the commitments they made in the Conference would be completed.

The plan was completed successfully and a letter was sent out to inform all the participants. Shortly thereafter, I received a call from the victim. He told me he left the Conference feeling it wouldn't work. He felt the process was good, but went on to tell me that he had been a public servant his entire working career. He said the last thing a government department did was work cooperatively with another department or community organization, and it was this experience that led him to believe the plan would fail.

The plan relied on four government departments and two community organizations working cooperatively together. He was impressed that the conferencing process had the strength to overcome these long-established barriers.

The following is a recommended four-part format.

Part 1: System issues

Specify what the Conference is requesting of the agency having jurisdiction, e.g., police, prosecutor, or court. For instance, the outcomes may state that the police or the prosecutor have agreed not to take any further action if the plan is successfully completed, or that the Conference is recommending that charges be taken before the court. If the case is, or is to be, before the court, the plan could recommend how the matter is to be monitored by the court. It could state that the Conference requests that the court adjourn the matter until the agreed-upon plan is completed, and if the plan is successfully completed, the matters could be withdrawn or discharged without any formal record. Alternatively, if the case has been referred from court, the Conference could recommend the overall sentence in which they would like to see the plan included.

Part 2: Reparation

This part should record the outcomes which focus on the offender "putting right" for the victim and community. These are outcomes such as reparation, restitution, and community work. This allows the victim to see clearly what is being done for him/her and keeps the Conference focused on its main purpose.

Part 3: Prevention

This part contains the outcomes that address the underlying causes for the offending and are aimed at assisting the offender to keep his/her promises to the victim. As examples, outcomes here could include drug and alcohol counseling, family counseling, or supervision contracts.

Part 4: Monitoring

The monitoring of the Family Group Conference plan is as important as any other part of the FGC process. Adults and/or organizations giving support to the plan must have the tenacity to see the plan through to its conclusion. In most cases where a plan fails, it is the supervising adults who fail to carry through.

The plan should specify just who is monitoring what, to whom they are to report, and what deadlines exist for each part of the plan. The best way to achieve good monitoring is to share the responsibility and write particular assignments into each individual outcome. In the final section of the plan, record to whom each monitoring person will report as each part is completed. It is a good practice to record how often the monitoring person(s) will make contact with the young person to check progress.

Let us repeat, monitoring is greatly assisted if the outcomes are measurable. Be sure to specify who, when, where, and how much. Recording when a particular outcome will start and the date it is due to be completed will greatly enable the monitoring process.

Avoid outcomes that say "reasonable" (reasonable to whom?) and have other unclear requirements, in order to escape debates about whether the spirit of the plan was completed or not.

Put as much responsibility as possible on the offending young person and his/her family. Remember that one of the principles is to foster the ability of the family to develop its own means of dealing with a child or young person of theirs who offends.

Note that when the youth has successfully completed the plan, all the participants are to be notified. If a closing meeting or celebration is included in the plan, this should now be arranged.

Extending the family

The FGC process has worked best when it has drawn upon the extended family and/or community support for the offender's family. Following are some suggestions about how to help this to happen.

The *extended family* should always be the first resource to be considered. However, some extended families are unable to be the resource that is required. This may be due to a number of reasons, including age, distance, illness, or the fact that they have their hands full with other members of the family. For a variety of causes, then, families may need help beyond their own resources, and this is one area where the process may need to be enhanced. Otherwise, one or both of the following two situations is likely to occur.

The first is that the process will require the family to open up its baggage for all to see, resulting in shame that will prove destructive and add to the family's sense of failure. The most likely outcome of this will be that the young person and his/her family will make commitments and promises that they feel obligated to make but will never be able to fulfill. The process could set them up to fail without benefiting anyone.

The second possibility is that the Conference will make concessions so that the outcomes are achievable. But the victim will bear most of the cost of these less productive outcomes. A family that can barely meet their day-to-day living costs may be able to agree to only minimal reparation. Compare that to an outcome in one case where the family not only met the reparation cost, but also gave each of the two victims a gift of a thousand dollars within four weeks. The extended family and their community raised the money through running sausage sizzles, car washes, and a stall at the local market. The young person in turn was committed to assist that group to fundraise for the next year. The network of support made it possible for this offender and his family to fully meet, and even go beyond, their obligation to the victim.

For these reasons, it is important to have a network of support available for offenders' families. The network needs to have variety and choice for the family. This network can be used to spread the burden in all aspects of the process for the family. Community groups can provide a number of resources to assist in the implementation and monitoring of the plan. Often they have services and programs that can be offered to the family, and, because they have the potential to be culturally appropriate, they can also provide helpful role models for the offender and his/her family.

Restorative justice is a community-building process.

5.

Beyond the Family Group Conference

My (Allan's) experience in Wellington and elsewhere has demonstrated that Family Group Conferences are most effective as part of a community-wide effort. This requires that community groups and organizations not only be drawn into the Conferences and their follow-up, but that they also be made part of an effort to address the patterns of youth offending in general.

Involving community groups as part of the overall Conference process gives them an opportunity to work in a co-operative way that will enhance their effectiveness, avoid duplication of services, and enable them to provide a "no gaps" service to the offending young person and his/her family. Their understanding of the commitments the young person and his/her family are required to make often further enhances the organization's effectiveness.

Funding for community initiatives is often spread very lightly through the community. Experience shows that when community agencies work together in the FGC process, they establish relationships that enable them to continue working together and to use their resources more effectively.

Conferencing the Conferences

The effectiveness of these community groups can be increased by "conferencing the results of the Conferences." The Coordinators who are involved in these Conferences, along with the police, are often able to see patterns and trends in the communities which are leading to youth offending. By helping community groups to come together and address these patterns that contribute to crime, Coordinators can spearhead the development of prevention strategies.

In one Conference, the facilitator asked me to be support for the victim because he and his mother were alone. The son had been brutally beaten. Neither the victim nor his mother wanted to be at the Conference with the offender.

The offending youth's family, of mixed heritage, was at odds with each other. They argued continually among themselves in front of the Conference. During the victim's time to speak, the offending youth's mother felt her son was being verbally attacked. The facilitator made an appropriate statement to the youth's mother, and then calmed the group enough to continue.

But, after a very lengthy family alone time, there was a huge change. The offender's family had worked together and created a workable, just plan. The youth and his family also apologized sincerely for what had happened to the woman's son. I remember the relaxed, smiling face of the victim's mother as she spoke to the facilitator and me after the Conference, saying that she experienced justice and hope, and that now she and her son could put this ugly incident behind them.

— An anonymous observer

Community groups who address causes, combined with the close collaboration of the Youth Aid Officers (the "youth police") and the Youth Justice Coordinator, account for the dramatic results in reducing youth crime achieved in Wellington, the capital city of New Zealand, over a three-year period and beyond. In Wellington, we (Allan and others) were able to identify the common factors among a group of youth who were accounting for 58% of youth court appearances.

Among these was a tendency for young Maori offenders to be out of touch with their heritage and community. Because of what we had learned in FGCs, we were uniquely able to assist a Maori community-service organization to develop a proposal which addressed the factors that were contributing to their young people's offending. We were also able to provide information to potential funding agencies about why it was important to underwrite the initiative. The proposal was financed, and a six-month program was implemented. The results of the well-focused initiative were astounding: the offending group disappeared totally from our court statistics. The number of burglaries and car thefts in Wellington dropped dramatically within the six-month term of the program and has remained low.

Another example of "conferencing the Conferences" involved addressing peer group issues. Parents often find they are competing against peer influences, and so do the plans that come out of an FGC. I would often witness genuine remorse and commitment from the young person at the end of the Conference, but within weeks I would see that commitment being undermined by his/her peer group. I also noted that most of the peer group came through FGCs for offending in similar ways. I realized we did not need to wait for each youth to come through individually. Within three Conferences we would know who the peer group was. They were mainly identified on the non-association lists (lists of young people the family wants its child to avoid) the parents put forward because of the negative influence the parents believed they had on their child/young person.

Once I had sufficient information about the issues that were contributing to the youth offending within the community, I asked the appropriate community agencies to

A young 13- or 14-year-old girl of Samoan-White heritage, who lived on the streets, had attempted to steal a woman's purse. The FGC for this case had about 40 people in attendance. The girl was obviously distraught. She was hunched over and dazed, and the sadness from her body seemed to permeate the whole room. Her Samoan mother, with breast-cancer, was in Australia. Her father, married sister, and adult family friends were present, along with social workers, the police, and others. Her "aunties" from the Samoan side of her family were there, as was her cultural community, including elders who could hardly move. Yet they were there to support her.

The FGC spent a very long time together during the family caucus. When we all reassembled to hear the plan they came up with, the group encouraged the girl to present it. Upon returning to the Conference circle, the girl physically looked like a different person. She was vibrant. She not only presented the plan well, she, and now everyone there, laughed and joked. The entire group showed genuine care for this beautiful child. It was a blessing to see.

— An anonymous observer

One evening I accompanied a facilitator to an evening meeting at a local cultural center. Before the meeting started, we ate and socialized. A young man came over and sat down beside me. He introduced himself. Through our conversation, I told him that I was there to study the FGC process. He said, "Oh, yeah, I've been to a few of those."

I said, "Really, could you tell me about them?"

He said casually, "They were FGCs for *me*."

Then he went on to praise the process and said that the FGCs turned him around. He said he did a lot of cultural work now, had a wonderful wife and baby, and a job he was proud of. I asked what he did. He said he was in the janitorial maintenance field. I said it sounded as if he'd found the right job. He said, "I absolutely have. I work at McDonald's, I do all the cleaning—tables, floors, toilets. I love it."

He made me feel that with that kind of sincerity and sense of self-worth, he'll probably own a few McDonald's before he's finished. Here he had run with the wolves, and now he's running with life.

— An anonymous observer

come together in a series of meetings.

The agencies I asked to meet included four or more community groups, the police, and education providers. I shared the profile I had on the offending group and facilitated the other participants in sharing their knowledge. The process of the meeting was nearly the same as many FGCs follow: information-sharing with the community groups, allowing them time to deliberate among themselves and prepare suggestions, and then the facilitated negotiation towards an agreement. At the end of the meeting we had an outline of a plan. I took this away and turned it into a draft proposal. I then reconvened the meeting after the participating groups had a chance to look at the draft proposal. From the second meeting, I obtained the information I needed to finalize the proposal and gain the groups' commitment to it.

The last step was to advocate for any extra resources that were required to put the proposals into an action plan. These were a lot easier to fund than the usual proposals, because at this point they already had government, agency, community, and police support.

Through this combined community-based strategy, we had marshalled support for the whole peer group to make changes. It was not long before the peer groups started supporting each other in positive ways and the negative influence disappeared from the Conference process. We had also created a program to which we can refer youth and their families.

In working this way, community groups have gained extra resources and experience, making them more effective for future Family Group Conferences. This is not just a short-term benefit, because their reputations are enhanced and funding agencies are more prepared to finance them. As Coordinator I am able to advocate better for them, because I can quote clear achievements that are supported by unmistakably positive statistics. The community groups have also gained a better understanding of what services are required and how they can be made user-friendly for youth. This has led to some major service delivery changes that have proven valuable in empowering families and have also made the community organizations excellent monitors of Conference plans.

Within a three-year period, Wellington experienced about a two-thirds drop in youth offending. In 1996, we addressed 554 charges. In 1999, we addressed 174. The number of Conferences required dropped over the same period from 160 to 78. We believe it was due to three main factors: effective Family Group Conferences, close working between the police and the Youth Justice Coordinator, and a collaborative, community-based initiative to address the causes of offending behavior.

Conferencing is not a soft option; it was introduced to New Zealand as tough justice. It has been highly successful.

A story

I (Allan) held a Conference for a young person who was a refugee. He had come to New Zealand with his grandmother, who was his caregiver, and an aunt. New Zealand had only just started taking refugees from this young man's country, so there were no other family members and, in fact, few other residents of his culture nearby. The three arrived in New Zealand with nothing but what they could carry. Their only income was from a benefit paid by the New Zealand government, which provided for only the very basics of food and accommodation.

The charge was serious; the young person had assaulted his grandmother for cash. He had taken the rent money, and the grandmother was afraid of what would happen now that she could not pay it. In desperation, she reported the incident to the aunt, who in turn reported it to the police.

The police referred the case to an FGC without making an arrest. I met with the grandmother and aunt to consult on what format the Conference might follow and, in particular, what cultural and/or religious process should guide it. In this meeting I learned that the grandmother had been assaulted on more than one occasion and that she did not know where to go for assistance.

I met with the young person to explain the process to him and to see if he could identify any possible supports. It was agreed that I would invite his teacher, but it was clear this was not going to be enough. I contacted two organizations: Victims as Survivors, and the Refugee and Migrants Services Trust. Neither organization had been involved with Family Group Conferencing but agreed to assist. I asked one to be the direct support for the grandmother and the other to help the young person meet his obligations to his grandmother.

I then arranged for the grandmother to meet with the supporting organization so that she could share her story with them. They, in turn, would help her share her story at the Conference. I advised the grandmother that they would also transport her to the Conference and see her safely back home. And I also arranged for the young person to meet with his supporting organization. They agreed that they would assist him in developing a plan to put things right and support him to complete it.

The Conference started with a prayer in their native language, and all parties used interpreters to ensure full understanding. The grandmother told her story in much detail, as did the young person. As the young person began to understand the impact he was having on his grandmother, tears came to his eyes. The young man eventually told of his life in a refugee camp before the three arrived in New Zealand, what he had to do to survive, and how in his new community he felt he could not mix with others if he did not have money. Clearly, loneliness, anger, and hurt were shared by both the young man and his grandmother.

The plan that came out of the Conference required the young person to pay in full all the money he had taken. He was given help to find part-time employment. It was agreed that he could not live with his grandmother until she felt safe with him in the house. The plan provided also for counseling to help him overcome the anger that he carried from his experiences in the refugee camp. A mentor was found from his own culture who would check that he kept his promises and put things right with his grandmother. The putting right called for him to cook a meal for his grandmother and to make an apology. He was also required to complete community work and attend school every day. He would receive support with his homework.

The plan was successful. The young man did no further offending, and he completed all his outcomes. Most valuable of all, both he and his grandmother found new friends and support that stayed with them, well beyond the Family Group Conference plan, and assisted them in starting their new lives in New Zealand.

Selected Readings

Books:

Hayden, Anne. *Restorative Conferencing Manual of Aotearoa New Zealand.* Dept. for Courts, New Zealand, 2001. (Orders may be placed through Anne Molloy, anne.molloy@courts.govt.nz.)

Brown, B.J. and F.W.M McElrea, eds. *The Youth Court in New Zealand: A New Model of Justice.* Legal Research Foundation, New Zealand, 1993. (Orders may be placed through Jane Kilgour at j.kilgour@auckland.ac.nz)

Galaway, Burt et. al., eds. *Family Group Conferences: Perspectives on Policy and Practice.* Criminal Justice Press, 1995.

Internet:

http://ssw.che.umn.edu/rjp/Resources/Resource.htm#Research Findings

http://www.iirp.org/library/fgcseries01.html

http://www.iirp.org/library/fgcseries02.html

http://www.restorativejustice.org

Books on restorative justice:

Consedine, Jim. *Restorative Justice: Healing the Effects of Crime.* Plowshares, New Zealand, 2nd edition, 1999.

Johnstone, Gerry. *Restorative Justice: Ideas, Values, and Debates.* Willam Publishing, UK, 2002.

Zehr, Howard. *Changing Lenses: A New Focus for Crime and Justice.* Herald Press, 1990/95.

Zehr, Howard. *The Little Book of Restorative Justice.* Good Books, 2002.

Acknowledgments

I wish to acknowledge those who assisted with the work reflected in this book. First, I must acknowledge the Maori people and, in particular, those involved with Kahungunu Ki Poneke Community Services and Mokai Kainga Maori Centre. Their guidance and support of young people have constantly inspired me.

I acknowledge the Wellington Youth Aid Service of the New Zealand Police for working in partnership with my position to develop the best practice model available throughout New Zealand. Their participation in Family Group Conferences and their commitment to the plans that came out of the process contributed greatly to the model's success.

I acknowledge Judge Henwood. She allowed and encouraged the working model to flourish in Wellington through partnership, coordination, and cooperation.

Lastly, I acknowledge KPMG Consulting who recognized and promoted the importance of the work in Wellington. They gave the model the National Supreme Award for Innovation that honored all who participated in its development.

— Allan MacRae

We also wish to thank the following for their suggestions on various drafts of the manuscript: Dee Tompkins, Carl Stauffer, Bonnie Price Lofton, Jarem Sawatsky, Rita Hatfield, Jessalyn Nash, and Judge FWM McElrea. In spite of all this feedback, however, we take full responsibility for the views and for any inaccuracies in this book.

— Allan MacRae and Howard Zehr

Appendices
Research and Statistics

National Research

In June, 2003, New Zealand researcher Gabriel Maxwell released the results of a major research project following up 1003 young people in New Zealand who had FGCs in 1998, with additional data from other cases. The following summarizes some of the conclusions of this study:

- The number of cases going to Youth Court has dropped dramatically since the introduction of the 1989 Act, from 600 per 10,000 cases in Youth Court in 1987, to about 250 per 10,000 in 2001.

- Cases resulting in incarceration of young people have also dropped significantly, from about 300 in 1987 to well under 100 in 2001.

- Almost all FGCs (90%) contained measures to ensure young offenders' accountability, and in over 80% of the cases the required tasks were successfully completed. Eighty percent of the accountability plans included repair of harm that had been caused.

- About half of the plans included measures to enhance the well-being of the young person—rehabilitative and/or reintegrative.

- The process goals of ensuring that appropriate people—including victims and families—participate, and that a consensus process be used, appear to be largely achieved. Not all victims attended, but that was mainly because not all chose to do so.

- Since participating in an FGC, most of the young people were able to develop positive goals and achieve successes, although some did continue to have negative life experiences and to re-offend. Other research cited suggests that if more good quality programs were provided as follow-up to the conferences, outcomes would be even more positive.

- Over the years since the introduction of the 1989 Act, the youth justice system has continued to grow in strength and has become more restorative. As part of this, the police have developed their own diversionary practices that reflect restorative rather than punitive philosophies. Similarly, the Youth Court appears to have become more inclusive. Victims more often appear to feel positively than in the early years. Reintegrative and rehabilitative programs are being offered to young offenders as well.

  At the same time, there is considerable room for improvement in practice, e.g., in increasing participation and consensus, in addressing cultural issues, and in reducing reliance on Youth Court.

"The research demonstrates that the nature of the youth justice process does affect critical outcomes for young people: both in terms of reducing offending and increasing the possibility of other positive life outcomes. Restorative practices that include empowerment, the repair of harm, and reintegrative outcomes make a positive difference, while the extent of embeddedness in the criminal justice system, severe and retributive outcomes, and stigmatic shaming have negative effects."

— Gabriel Maxwell
June, 2003

Benefits of Family Group Conferences

For victims

Victims who participate in FGCs have a chance to tell their offenders about the impact the offenses have on them. By meeting with offenders they gain a better understanding of what happened and why. They also have an opportunity to identify what they need in order for things to be put right. As is true of restorative justice programs elsewhere, a higher proportion of reparation is collected for victims when it is agreed to through a Conference rather than when it is simply court-ordered. Victims often find their offenders less intimidating after meeting with them, leading to an increased sense of safety. Often the victims are linked with support that they have not been aware of until informed of their rights as part of the Conference convening process. Overall, involvement in the FGC process contributes to a sense of empowerment for victims.

For the young person

In addition to having a better understanding of the impact of his/her behavior, the youth has the opportunity to earn back respect, to develop under the guidance of appropriate adult role models, and to maintain and develop the skills required for living successfully within a community. Opportunities can be provided for the youth to move into a more positive peer group and to be linked to his/her cultural community for support and guidance. Cultural supports have proven to be the most effective at getting the child/youth to complete his/her obligations to the victim.

For the offending youth's family

The family can be supported to be more effective, both with the child/youth that has offended and with other siblings. The family has the opportunity to remove the shame and sense of failure that comes through the offending committed by its family member. The family often gains long-term support networks. Isolated families can be linked to their residential and cultural communities.

For the community

The FGC process provides information that can empower the community to effectively address issues that contribute to offending within their community. FGCs promote closer and more effective relationships between government and community agencies. The process offers less costly responses. In New Zealand, millions have been saved in custody and court costs. The process provides the community with a greater opportunity to be involved, allows members of the community to be recognized as victims, and provides a way for the community to take appropriate responsibility for its members.

For the police

The FGC process empowers the police to seek appropriate outcomes. They gain substantially greater information about the community which they police, leading them to be better prepared to use their resources more effectively. FGCs help the police build a closer and more effective relationship with youth, their families, and their community, and to be better respected by those with whom they deal.

Sample Proposal to Address Peer Groups

Following is a basic outline of a proposal to address peer group issues. The proposal was developed to address the underlying causes of inappropriate behavior among a specific group of young people in Wellington. Not all had been charged with offending, but some had, and we strongly suspected that they all were involved in the same activities.

We expected to see these young people continue to be charged with further offending, but once this proposal was enacted, not one had another Conference, nor did any appear in court over the next three years while I was in Wellington. The project cost $14,000 New Zealand dollars. The proposal worked because it identified needs and matched up resources through an extended Conference process. *This was a program built around the needs of a specific group rather than forcing the group to fit within the needs of a program.*

A. Issues that were addressed in the proposal:
   a. Drug and/or alcohol abuse.
   b. Living outside the education system; truancy.
   c. Little or no networks in the community; not feeling part of their community or culture.
   d. No or inappropriate adult role models.
   e. Anger because of suffering some form of trauma, mainly through physical or mental abuse.

B. The plan for the Maori youth included:
   1. Group work on drug and alcohol abuse.
   2. Learning Maori songs and traditional dances.
   3. Learning a life skills program, including moving towards independence.
   4. Activities that put them in contact with support people in their immediate communities and their culture.
   5. Anger management.
   6. Driving lessons provided by the police.
   7. First Aid course funded by the police.
   8. Support, assistance, and education for parents.
C. The proposal had the following goals:
   1. All youth would be in formal education or be employed at the end of six months.
   2. The group would participate in the Ratana Church celebrations that would be held in the full Maori tradition. This goal required many hours of team training and practice.
   3. The youth would complete a three-day canoe trip to celebrate their achievement of the above goals.

Types of FGCs in New Zealand

There are four types of FGCs for youth offenders.

- *Intention to Charge Conference.* In this Conference, the police have decided they are prepared to charge the young person, but the youth is not under arrest. The Conference explores the resources available to it and whether the matter can be addressed without going to court. If it is agreed that the matter should go to court, the Conference will make a recommendation that the enforcement agency should prosecute (lay the charges in court). If the Conference cannot reach agreement, the enforcement agency is free to proceed to court with the matter.

- *Custody Conference.* This Conference is automatically held when the court places a young person who has denied an offense in custody. This Conference is held to explore other options besides custody. If it is agreed that the young person should stay in custody, the FGC decides what sort of programs should occur for that young person while s/he is in custody. This Conference helps ensure that families have say over what happens for the young person.

- *Charge Not Denied Conference.* When a young person appears in court s/he is asked if s/he takes some responsibility for what occurred. This is usually done through the youth's advocate, a court-appointed lawyer, who indicates that the charge is not denied. This is not a formal plea of guilty. In these cases the court must direct an FGC to recommend how the charges could be handled. The Conference could agree to a recommendation that the charges be withdrawn from court, have a young person complete a plan while on remand, with or without bail conditions, and/or discharge the charges as if they were never laid in court. Alternatively, the FGC can recommend to the court what orders it should make and the plans for those orders. This Conference could also recommend that charges be amended to more accurately reflect the incident. On very serious charges, the Conference also recommends in what jurisdiction the case should be handled—Youth Court or District (adult) Court.

- *Charge Proven Conference.* The court calls for this Conference after a defended court hearing has found the young person guilty. In New Zealand, a Conference must be held before a court makes orders or sentences a young person. This applies to all charges other than murder or manslaughter. The Conference is convened to make recommendations to the court on the sentence or alternative outcomes.

About the Authors

Allan MacRae is Manager of Coordinators for the Southern Region of New Zealand, overseeing Family Group Conferences for both Youth Justice, and Care and Protection. Prior to taking this position, he was Youth Justice Coordinator for the capital city of Wellington.

After receiving the National Supreme Award for Innovation, Allan developed a program in Wellington which emerged as a leading model of Youth Justice. Subsequently, he was a lead trainer in the "Best Practice Road Show," designed to bring these practices to other areas of New Zealand. He has also conducted numerous trainings in Belgium, Thailand, and the United States.

Allan received his diploma in Social Work from Victoria University and has 23 years of experience working with young offenders and at-risk youth.

Howard Zehr is considered a founder of the field of restorative justice. He lectures, trains, and consults internationally, including in New Zealand. His book *Changing Lenses: A New Focus for Crime and Justice* is considered a classic in the field.

Other publications include *Doing Life: Reflections of Men and Women Serving Life Sentences; Transcending: Reflections of Crime Victims;* and *The Little Book of Restorative Justice.* He is Co-Director of the graduate Center for Justice and Peacebuilding at Eastern Mennonite University (Harrisonburg, Virginia).

In 2003 he received the Annual PeaceBuilder Award from the New York Dispute Resolution Association and the Restorative Justice Prize from Prison Fellowship International "for significant contributions to the advancement of Restorative Justice around the world."

Howard received his B.A. from Morehouse College and his Ph.D. from Rutgers University.

METHOD OF PAYMENT

☐   Check or Money Order
*(payable to **Good Books** in U.S. funds)*

☐   Please charge my:
    ☐ MasterCard   ☐ Visa
    ☐ Discover   ☐ American Express

\# _____

exp. date _____

Signature _____

Name _____

Address _____

City _____

State _____

Zip _____

Phone _____

Email _____

SHIP TO: (if different)

Name _____

Address _____

City _____

State _____

Zip _____

Mail order to: **Good Books**
P.O. Box 419 • Intercourse, PA 17534-0419
Call toll-free: 800/762-7171
Fax toll-free: 888/768-3433
Prices subject to change.

Group Discounts for

The Little Book of
Family Group Conferences
ORDER FORM

If you would like to order multiple copies of
The Little Book of Family Group Conferences by
Allan MacRae and Howard Zehr for groups you know
or are a part of, use this form. (Discounts apply only
for more than one copy.)

Photocopy this page as often as you like.

The following discounts apply:	
1 copy	$4.95
2-5 copies	$4.45 each (a 10% discount)
6-10 copies	$4.20 each (a 15% discount)
11-20 copies	$3.96 each (a 20% discount)
21-99 copies	$3.45 each (a 30% discount)
100 or more	$2.97 each (a 40% discount)

Prices subject to change.

Quantity   *Price*   *Total*

_____ copies of *Family Group Conferences* @ _____ _____

PA residents add 6% sales tax _____

Shipping & Handling
(add 10%; $3.00 minimum) _____

TOTAL _____